# Echoes of Light

# Contents

The poets who have contributed to this volume are listed below, along with the relevant page upon which their work can be found.

| | | | |
|---|---|---|---|
| 74 | Stella Backham | | Rita Laundon |
| 75 | Daniel Riggs | 114 | Kevin Power |
| 76 | Irene Bishop | | Frances Jessup |
| 77 | Tracy Verrall | 115 | A Cleary |
| 78 | Graeme Allan | 116 | A A Marcoff |
| 79 | Diane Jones | | L Dale |
| 80 | Matt Rowley | 117 | Gladys C'Ailceta |
| 81 | Matthew Hawkins | | Dave Benham |
| | Rose L Pearce | 118 | Marina O'Shea |
| 82 | E M Woodford | | Rowland Scannell |
| 83 | Peter Bauer | | E Cornish |
| 84 | Frederick Seymour | 119 | Van Scharer |
| 85 | Emma Neale | | Richard Jones |
| 86 | Jean Smith | 120 | Marjorie Wagg |
| 87 | Helen Gust | | Linda Finch |
| 88 | G J Jenkins | 121 | Tessa Box |
| 89 | M Clifton | | N Kerry |
| 90 | Rone | 122 | Michael Rowson |
| 91 | Anna Parkhurst | | Claire Shadwell |
| 92 | Ken Smith | 123 | Laurie Hilton-Ash |
| 93 | N Radford | | K Bailes |
| | Jean Walker | 124 | Sylvia Ash |
| 94 | Tilly Timbrell-Sturgeon | | Suzanne Mudd |
| 95 | Julia Ziewe | 125 | Clive Marks |
| 96 | iam | | Iris Owen |
| 97 | Jasmine Bates | 126 | Alan Lavender |
| | J R Wheeler | | Julie Sexton |
| 98 | L W Baker | 127 | Tom Chilton |
| 99 | Carole Raymond | | J A Karpinska |
| 100 | Ron Dean | 128 | Ms Kerry |
| 101 | Carole Fendt | | J Fermor |
| | Thomas Victor Healey | 129 | June Pledger |
| 102 | E Root | | Vanessa Galloway |
| | R Louis | | |
| 103 | Carol Starkey | | |
| 104 | Geraldine Foy | | |
| 105 | Nerine Selwood | | |
| 106 | Doreen Blake | | |
| 107 | P J De-Gutis | | |
| 108 | Leslie Hawkins | | |
| 109 | Barbara Geraghty | | |
| 110 | Terence Richardson | | |
| 111 | C Mappley | | |
| | Ruth Daviat | | |
| 112 | Debbie Gadd | | |
| | Bewick Wilson | | |
| 113 | Elizabeth Woodhouse | | |

# Foreword

In these days of cynicism and mammon-worship, it's a delight for me to be associated with a volume of poetry like "Echoes of Light". The publishing industry has all but turned its back on limited interest subjects like poetry and gone off in hot pursuit of the next bestseller like a dog chasing ambulances. Publishing was once a noble profession, guided by people with ideals. Now it's just another business more interested in profit margins than prophets. In these times when the industry seems to do nothing but produce banal historical sagas, formula thrillers and "Ten easy lessons to improve your public image" books, there is little room for new writers with something to say about life in the raw. Thirty years ago these same publishers were falling over themselves to seek out talented new novelists and poets with something interesting to say about the human predicament. "Echoes of Light" is one tiny shaft of light in the darkness. It gives an opportunity to poets to express themselves in print - many for the first time ever (but I hope, not the last). The subjects of these poems are as diverse and individual as the poets themselves. Read through its pages and consider, without poetry we would be a sorry excuse for a civilisation. If this book inspires one person to pick up a pen and set down his or her thoughts, it has, at least, done something to rage against the dying of the light.

*Peter Quinn, Editor.*

This edition featuring the work of poets from the
South East Counties of Greater London, Surrey,
West Sussex, East Sussex, Essex and Kent

ISBN 0-9509587-8-6

First published in Great Britain in 1999 by
BYWORD
1 Yorke Street
Burnley
BB11 1HD
Tel: 01282 459533
Fax: 01282 412679
ISBN for complete set of volumes
0-9509587-6-X
All Rights Reserved

Copyright contributors 1999


*Cover photo by courtesy of*
*North West Tourist Board*

TONIGHT

Moonlight crisp once more
From outside the closed in shadowed door
Everything is still and calm
So nothing can come to harm
As small drop swiftly drop from the sky
Like tears from a baby's eye
Once more the storm approaches our summer bay
Like a strong voice commanding, stay away
Everything that does exist is now blown into the strong
mist
Now tonight is slowly going and today is horizing
The sun spreads round the darkened sky
So beautiful, which even money can't buy

*Donna Givan, Southall*

Born in Northern Ireland **Donna Givan** is just 13-years-old.
"I began writing poetry when I was ten," said Donna. "I
enjoy writing as it allows me to be creative and helps me to
relax." She is influenced by natural life and her surround-
ings and described her style as peaceful and tranquil. Her
hobbies include poetry, dancing and arts and crafts. "My
ambition is to swim with bottled-nosed dolphins under the
sunset and I would love to live in America," she said.

# TREASURES OF THE COUNTRYSIDE

If you live in the countryside
You are very rich
King cups are your pot of gold
They grow around the ditch

Emeralds are your bright green fields
Where mushrooms are found at dawn
Poppies are your rubies
Which grow amongst the corn

Daisies are your silver
Little chains we make
Sapphire are the milkmaids
They grow around the lake

Diamonds the raindrops
On the wild rose and thorn
To hear the chorus of the birds
That sing when it is dawn

*Mary Simpson, Wickford*

Born in Kent **Mary Simpson**, author of "Treasures of the Countryside" now lives in Wickford. "I started writing poems several years ago for recreation," she explained. "I am influenced by things around me and my style is rustic." A housewife, she is married to John and has one child. She keeps show dogs and her hobbies include dog shows and gardening. "I have written many poems but this is the first one I have had published," she said. She is interested in ecology and would like to meet David Bellamy. " My worst nightmare is for our greenbelt area to be taken over for building work," she said.

# UNSEEN

A happy, contented group is a joy to see
But a friend is needed, oh lonely me
Loneliness gathers around me like a shroud
Separates me from a bustling crowd
A cry in the dark, who is there to hear
A loneliness hard to witness, let alone share
Friends are needed, shall they listen
Or wish to look behind the eyes where hidden tears glisten
So I'll summon a smile, and join them to sit outside
Being lonely in a crowd is so easy to hide

*Patricia Dawson, Sandwich*

**Patricia Dawson** has written children's short stories and many poems but this is the first time she has gone into publication. Born in High Minster, she started writing two years ago for therapy. "I would like to remembered with love and care by my family and if possible as an artist and poet," she said. Aged 66, she has been married to James for 44 years and has two children and two grandchildren plus a dog, a cat, and rabbits. Her hobbies include drawing, artwork, gardening and cooking.

# I DREAMT OF DARKENED SKIES

I dreamt of darkened skies
And young girls cries
Of furry bunnies
Hanging on razor blade trees
Thank God for my lobotomy

I dreamt of salt on the wind
Glad that I had not sinned
Of raging sea, a clear blue day
I know I've had to pay my way

I dream of nothing, nothing all is black
Oh Lord
Please forgive me
And give me
My little piece Of brain back

*Andrew Iles, St Leonards-On-Sea*

# FOREVER

At night as I drift into my sleep and into darkness really deep
My mind goes to a secret place where I hear your laugh and see your face
My mind and thoughts go to a shrine where I do pray that you'll be mine
My thoughts light a candle that's clear and bright and my love for you burns through the night
For no one knows about this place, this shrine I've built to you in space
No one else has ever been there, only now with you this secret I share
Our love is special, so deep and true together we are one, apart we are two
So many years have now passed by and things we said and tears we'd cry
Not all our times were good just bad and throughout the years so many were sad
But our love has stood the test of time in this world or the next, one day you'll be mine
If I have to wait, then that I will do for our love for each other will always shine through
And when our time on earth is finally done and we walk together towards the sun
Our spirits will rise up oh so high, and our souls will become bright stars in the sky
Our fathers long gone will show us the way and we'll turn to each other and we will say
Together forever that's what we will be I'll say I love you and you'll say you love me

*Jay Colman, Colchester*

A POEM

A hermit, name of Edward Dear
Forgot 'twas Christmas time one year
He didn't have a single treat
No rum to drink, no cakes to eat
He didn't have a nut to crack
No garlands bright adorned his shack
And all because no one had taught him
That Christmas comes at end of autumn

Now later, near the end of May
It snowed quite hard one freezing day
And when dear Edward saw the snow
He thought, "Now where did Christmas go?
I'd quite forgotten all about it
But don't intend to go without it"
And so he had his first Christmas fling
When it was near the end of spring

*Charmaine Bourton, Croydon*

THE DAY I SAW A MONSTER

I saw a monster outside my bedroom last night
At the sight it gave me such a fright

I had a dream about monsters last night
I imagined them green, purple, red and slimy, eyes bright

How can I get monsters out of my mind?
Some are frightening, some are kind

You just can't tell

*Helen & Laura Almond, Brighton*

## PRIMARY SCHOOL TEACHER'S POEM

How does it feel being
Knee deep in children

Fussing around them like a
Sweet mother hen

You teach them to read
To write and to paint

The mess they all make
Leaves you feeling quite faint

At the end of the day
You are happy to say

"Little darlings, little darlings
I have given them my best"

"Now I need to put my feet up
And have a good rest"

You say to one another
"I'm feeling all in"
But
Tomorrow is another day
Just waiting to begin

*Mandy Golfin, E Sussex*

# THE FUTURE

I wonder what the future holds
If we could lift the hands of time
And peep beyond into fates fold
What mystery would we see?
What mountains must we climb?

Perhaps it's not purely chance
We can't unwrap tomorrow's treats
To have them for today and dance
Would leave a chasm at our feet

Just one thing I would ask of fate
In her kind recipe to designate
A spoonful of love to oil each day
So I wend with joy, life's tortuous way

*Yolande Clark, Clacton-On-Sea*

Dedicated to EJLSWF and my Rock for bequesting enthusiasm and energy, consideration and compassion coupled with inspiration and ingenuity.

**Yolande Clark** said: "I am a Life Fellow of the Royal Society of Arts, dubbed 'The Lady on the Bike' by Clacton locals due to my efforts to promote an 'inclusive' vision so locals are consulted. Strongly influenced by Shakespeare, Churchill and Christina Rossetti, I have been writing verse for 40 years as a means of trying to solve the puzzle of life. The activity I most enjoy is swimming in the sea with nieces, nephews, great nieces and great nephews, followed by cycling, dancing, writing, reading, crochet and classic cars. My retirement as Senior Lecturer provided an opportunity to do voluntary work and fund raising. My ambition is to help launch a new charity which would fund transport to visit loved ones in hospital or hospice. I have had articles published in the British Journal of Occupational Therapy on Information Technology."

# WOMEN

There she sat, face stony clad, with look of cosmic thunder
Was it something that I said, I just sit here and wonder
Was it something that I'd done or didn't do, you know
If you asked what's wrong my love, you get a grunt or
groan
Silence fills the air for hours, days or weeks, sometimes
You think whatever have you done, and yet there are no
signs
As time goes by you've tried your best, in making things
alright
A last approach to clear the air, she blows like dynamite
You know just what you've done she says, you don't need
me to tell
I don't, I don't, you plead to her, this is just like living hell
But in the end sanity does win, and she starts to talk again
You don't know why she's changed her mind, but knew you
couldn't win
Your just glad that it's over, and she is out your hair
It's back to normal once again, but how long can she spare
I'll never know the reason why until my dying day
Them funny things that ladies do, or don't do, or don't say

*Robert Farley, Sutton*

# THE WEATHERMEN

I felt compelled to venture out, the air was damp and cold
They forecast rain and gails today but still I won't be told
I walked for miles across open fields, looking upward to the sky
I felt the water lick my face and began to realise why

The weathermen are up there, I don't mean the presenters on TV
Who stand well groomed beside their charts informing you and
me
I think they work above us and have since time began
We share their moods every day, I'll explain it if I can

Contentment is a fine spring day, when all around us just feels
right
But a roar of disapproval? That's the thunder in the night
Sunshine never fails to lift us, I think the weathermen feel the
same
But what could be said of light showers, or worse, torrential rain

The snow at Christmas is peaceful, smothering all surrounding
sound
I've watched the sleet in winter though and hailstones shooting to
the ground
Although I've no ideas on hailstones as they really are quite odd
Surely blustery winds without question is the sighing of the Gods

And if they're really up there, providing wind, rain and shine
Then they deserve some recognition for their efforts all the time
So thank you for giving us the weather, without it where would we
be?
Thanks for the view from the window each day, for giving me so
much to see

*Lorraine Wood, Beddington*

# TITANIC

It was 1912, April, Wednesday the tenth
Titanic set sail to show all her strength
The ship left Southampton harbour in the late afternoon
So a few hours later they had the light of the moon
New York city is the place of their destination
And this was the best way to get a relaxing vacation
On 14th April, far out in the North Atlantic
The sea so smooth and very romantic
But late that night they had bad luck
Titanic was heading for an iceberg, then tragedy struck
The titanic crashed and made a big hole
Now people were praying for their soul
There was nothing they could do
It happened faster than a blink
Then in the cold Atlantic, Titanic began to sink
People started to cram up the lifeboats saving their lives
People got lost from their husbands, children and wives
Now people were stranded at sea, what were they to do?
But sure enough, help came to rescue the survivors and
crew

*Jason Warner, Worcester Park*

NEARLY NEW

Long rails of wedding dresses swing
Pale echoes of a festal day
What fate will speculators bring
Has all their glory fled away?

Still they command a special place
Apart from common coat and gown
Of honour there is still a trace
Commercial currents cannot drown

They clothed with glamour for an hour
Magnetic curve of breast and limb
How will they fare in wind and shower
Who will be wearing them next spring?

The bridal dress and more, will fade
Into the serried racks of time
Good looks and resolutions made
With years may falter and decline

And yet, like dresses on display
We hoard the best of all we know
The outward is what fades away
The inward will survive and grow

*John Adamson Brown, Carshalton*

**John Adamson Brown**, author of "Nearly New" writes poems on a
wide variety of subjects. Themes include human relationships,
art, spirituality and the use of words, with some humorous and
oblique approaches. A Baptist Minister who became a Social
Worker, he is married with two sons and two grandchildren. His
interests are group work, reading, art and world religions. John
has published in "Envoi", other magazines and various antholo-
gies. He said: "I am committed to the Christian Church and see a
great challenge and opportunity in applying its message to today's
needs. Poetry has its part in this."

PARK BENCH GARDEN

Well I've been gabbling...
Tea cups and TV,
And mutual friends
In lesser places, unthinkingly;
Not knowing that this would end
Or begin in a interrupted kiss.
Unaware of my own intentions,
And after hours of French,
And lawyers, cars and home,
Your cigarettes with the butts broken off
My caffeine habit (companion to suspect flip flops), a kiss.
Suspected by everyone but us
And then suspended by them.

*Frances Easter, Whitstable*

**Frances Easter** is from Whitstable, in Kent; a quaintly unique and tacky town, and the subject of much of her writing and painting. She has been writing poetry and prose for just over a year now, has two other poems being published this year, and has recently started a novel. "Park Bench Garden" is set in her best friend's back garden and describes the events of a party after last year's local regatta. She is ridiculed by her family, and friends for her love of handbags, The Supremes, peanut butter, and Shakespeare. She eventually hopes to write and act professionally.

## WE SHALL

If we shall live we live
If we shall die we die
If we live we will meet again
But tonight it's goodbye
One word, let but one word be heard

If we sleep we wake again
And see tomorrow's light
If we wake we shall meet again
But tonight it's goodbye

If we live we must part
If we die we part in pain
If we die we part only to meet again

To meet, worth living for
To meet, worth dying for
To meet, worth parting for
Never to part anymore

*Sonya B, Mitcham*

# DEATH BY POTASSIUM

I smile when the memory comes to mind
Of sitting behind the dirty glass screen
Listening to the erratic pops and fizzes
And the eerily bright purple light
Common to the substance
Then suddenly the potassium bursts forth
And there is an almighty bang
The hamster running on its wheel freezes
Time is frozen for an instant
Hours later he falls onto the soft sawdust
Beneath him
A victim of the unbelievable killer
Potassium

*Becky Butler, Barnes*

**Becky Butler** said: "I was born in south west London in 1982. I'm a pupil at the William Morris Academy, Fulham. My poems and articles have been published regularly since late 1995. I also give poetry readings and participate in creative writing workshops. I was runner up in a regional poetry competition to commemorate National Poetry Day in 1998. My poetry has recently been published on a website. The address is http://members.aol.com /seren 95931. I live in Barnes with my cats Stoffie and Midnight and my parents."

FORGIVE AND FORGET

Don't hit me with the rubber hammer
Of your forgiveness
With all the violence of its judgement
You meant it to be a soft blow
But it still strikes me

Take the bowl of your compassion
Fill it with the tears of your tenderness
And wash me with your love

Then pour it away
To water the future and drown the past

*Michael Sawyer, Hastings*

MUM

Strategic, quick thinking Sue
Alert and adjustable
Talkative
Stubborn, strong willed Sue
A magnet of jollidity
And a bringer of caring memories
And fun hours

A brain teaser and a player
Of knowledge and wit
A dictionary of words
A crossword player
A reader
And all the world to me

*C Lee-Rowden, Whitstable*

## SONNET TO THE WANDLE

Rushing past its leafy banks
Giving peace and beauty - thanks
Glinting in the bright sunlight
What an awe inspiring sight
The ducks are gathered on a isle
Cleaning and preening all the while
Suddenly it comes o'er cast
The heavens open with a blast
The rain pours down on stormy foam
The ducks go squawking off to home
The river rushes to the sea
Taking with it a broken tree
Then all is quiet along the banks
At last there's peace and beauty - thanks

*Alan Ridge, Cheam*

## HUMOUR IN VERSE

We took the kids to the zoo
And let them feed the goats
They looked lean and hungry too
We took the kids to the zoo
And came away with just their coats
They'll eat anything those goats
We took the kids to the zoo
And let them feed the goats

*Pat Sturgeon, Kent*

EARLY MORNING

How beautiful the trees, still and quiet in the dawning light
Tribute to their maker

On the roads the frantic race begins, get the car out, get it away
Another pound, another day

The trees stand still and quiet, serene in the morning light
Tribute to their maker

They have no time, they cannot see, the beauty of the red rose
light
Robins darting from the lofty height

The trees stand still and quiet, upwards looking in the morning
light
Tribute to their maker

What is the point of all this rush, oh money dictates, it must, it
must
It's not just a question of earning a crust

The trees stand still and quiet, aloof from man's continuous folly
Tribute to their maker

*Daphne McFadyen, Earlsfield*

**Daphne McFadyen** only began writing poetry recently "I did it as
a form of relaxation to get me through difficult situations," she
explained. "I write on subjects that are a part of my life and sus-
tain, console or amuse me and I find my inspiration from within,"
she said. A full-time carer, she is married to Alex and has three
children. Her hobbies include travelling, photography, dancing
and crosswords. "My ambition is to continue to travel and I par-
ticularly want to see India and Bonn to visit Beethoven's birth-
place." When we asked her who she would like to be for a day she
told us that she would enjoy being an extra in a costume drama.

# THE SCARECROW

Blowing in movement your swaying arms neither real or
alive
Your nodding head with no eyes
The sun is shedding its final shafts of fading gold
As the fingers of night draw on the cold
Shadows long now hide the corn
The whispering breezes as voices of old
As in silence the scarecrow faces another night alone

*Gary Smith, Eastbourne*

# INTERLUDE

I grasp the spiralled ring of
Black wrought iron
A single twist
And the heavy panelled door creaks open
I enter the hallowed portals
Silence
Broken only by the clang of metal on metal
As the latch slots into place
Behind me
Sanctuary
I stand immobile, my eyes scanning
The stone walls
Stone floor
The lofty wood - beamed roof
Its intricate carvings testimony of a craftsman's skill
I move forward
And my footsteps echo
Intrusive

*Joan Ashwell, Clacton-On-Sea*

# SONG IN AUTUMN

The spirits of the dead have arisen
And scaly slide up to light, like cobras
Lain long in forgotten burial chambers
Under bare arching branches, the wizen
Skeletal leaves fall, as sacrosanct streamers
The people gather these to a fiery furnace
Then fearing stand by as with menace
In red eyes the reborn God arrests dreamers

One drab October morn from slumber I awoke
And wandered to the shattered old church, where
                    between
The graves fungi the relics of flowers did choke
And the grubs of pestilential beetles were weaned
On carrion. In the church woodworm ate the oak
And collections strangled the congregation
But there, on the altar - the withered candles
                    flame
Soon to ignite advent, and a new life proclaim

*Gareth Davies, Hindhead*

# THE SHOPPING CENTRE

This shop sells transient beauty
Wrapped neatly in cellophane
But soon the blooms will wither
And we will need to go back again

This shop sells oblivion
In bottles of every size and shape
As time goes by need
More and more in order to escape

Many shops sell false pride
They pander to our vainest thought
But at the end of the day we realise
That it all adds up to nought

Where is the shop that sells happiness?
Where is the one that sells content?
And can the Citizens Advice Bureau
Tell me where my whole life went?

*K Shepherd, Maldon*

# THE HILL

Again I climbed the hill today
As oft we used to do
Where standing hand in hand
We always shared the view
If anyone was watching
They would think I was alone
Just flitting through old memories
Of places we had known
Gazing down across the lea
With every shade of green
From foliage into fields
For as far as can be seen
I felt a warm and gentle breeze
Softly caress my hair
And with each gentle movement
I knew that you were there
Reluctantly, I turned away
And wandered down the lane
Knowing I was not alone
But with you once again

*Maureen E Parmenter, Haslemere*

## SUNSHINE FUN

I'm lyin' on this Italian beach
The calamine is out of reach
See I'm burnt all red from head to toe
I feel embarrassed I'm all aglow

So I say to this fella with the white toothed grin
"I'm all on fire, got some cream for me skin?"
His teeth clattered yes, three mille lire
I said, "God blimey, that's far too dear"

So here I lay stuck in this groove
Me bits are so sore I daren't move
And all these bronze bodies pass gently by
Me, I lay stuck to the sand like a captured fly

*Diane-Marie Barton, Burgess Hill*

## SUMMER DEPARTURE

The tall trees like tall ships, weigh anchor
Rooted in their harbour of parkland
Harboured parkland
Awaiting their sailing time, leaf falling time
Not yet, not yet
Your embarking, your divesting
Marks summer departing
Stay, stay in all your glorious rigging
Proud ships, proud trees
Let us share your lovely array
Flags flying, leaves signalling

*Janice Squires, Eastbourne*

## MOTHER

What is a mother? Who can say?
She does so many jobs each day
Mother cooks for us our meal
Bathes our cuts to help them heal
Our clothes are washed and put away
She'll even find some time to play
If she asks what a day we've had
And we reply that it's been bad
She takes the time to sit us down
To let us tell her why we frown
If she can she'll put it right
Then tucks us in and says goodnight
She carries on with all her chores
Like polishing and cleaning floors
Then she washes up the plates
Is there any job she hates?
Even when some times are rough
A mother seems to be so tough
If you ask what pay she gets
She says it's done for love, my pets

*Christine Brown, Morden*

CHRISTMAS EVE

When all the children are sleeping soundly
And the milk and mince pies are left out
Santa Claus climbs down the chimney spreading gifts
throughout
With his little white beard and his big red suit
He climbs all the way back to the top
Where he meets his reindeer
He climbs in the sleigh
"Come on now boys, chop, chop"
He flies through the sky just beating time
Delivering all of his toys
To all of those millions of children down there
His little girls and boys

*Odette Golding, Ashford*

This poem is dedicated to my sister Leander and her son
Kai who died 05.09.98. My sister was my "Real
Inspiration"!

BALANCE

If we could weigh darkness
on Egyptian scales
Measure its heavy
oppressive presence
Would we find that its balance
was the richness of dreams?
A brocaded counterpane
warming the sleeping soul
Providing ballast?

*Hildi Mitchell, Brighton*

# UNTITLED

I can't seem to move
My limbs feel like lead
My grey cells consumed by fog
Bright sun casts but gloom in the dust covered room
That once used to pass for my head
Distemper piles high in the hair topped sky
Lethargic my life force seems nil
It's depression you say
Just subconscious at play
Not torpid and lazy but ill
I must see the sun for the light that it is
And open my heart to its ray
It's time to stop fearfully clinging to doom
And be rid of its menace some way
With the apathy shed
I can rise from my bed
But perhaps it'll not be today
There's a comfort in tears and in nurturing fears
That for some reason just won't go away

*Angela Storey, Northolt*

For my mum, without whom I couldn't rise.

**Angela Storey**, author of "Untitled" lives in Northolt with
her daughter Hannah and partner James. She has been
writing poems for 16 years and takes her inspiration from
the fickleness of human nature. "I started writing poems as
a child with my mother. She would start a limerick and I
would then complete the verse. It was a childhood game
that quickly grew into a passion," she explained. "To see
my words in print is a dream now fulfilled and I hope to
have further works published in the future."

# HUMAN RACE

Too many secrets whispered
Not enough stories told
I stand in the corner listening
As all the lies unfold

Too many unspoken words
Not enough love to go round
I stand there frozen listening
As all their lies mound

Too many people crying
Not enough reason to live
I stand far away listening
As all the lies start to give

Too many ways to die
Not enough care to exist
I stand outside looking in
As all the cries for help are missed

Too many feelings dying
Not enough peace in this place
I sink into the dread of despair
As will all the human race

*Lyndsey Coyne, Folkestone*

# THE PURPOSE

Let not this moment pass unfilled with sweetness
Regretting not a moment gone
Let not this creative time pass barren
With no seed to bloom in moments yet to come

The spectres of the past are but the shadows
That should have fled with new days dawn
Their being not to stay the sunrise
But the light reveal the reason they were born

Seeing within the path that led to sorrow
Regret will not its step retrace
But disclose the wonder of this moment
A womb to seed with love's more fulfiling grace

No time in creations holy breath but now
Cling not to that which is no more
Nor dream, nor yearn for that which will not be
Except its birth be through pain of suffering bore

So let each breathless moment be a new birth
Creation waits with baited breath
That you may send forth once more that thought
Blessing the sanctity of this moment's death

*Don Hatch, Grays*

# THE HUMBLE BEES

A wet spring, water-logged fields
And drenched couchant sheep are seen
From the slow train; scattered daffodils too
And little trees of fragile luminous green

In the retirement home December people
Eagerly glance, "Is this visitor for me?"
Helpers cheerful, too few, guide zimmer-walkers
Coax back the wanderers, serve the tea

Of those huddled, one headed a corporation
One ruled a hospital, somewhere far inside
Are hollows thick with primroses, and children
Who seldom come, forgetful, and friends who have died

Yet they hold on, they struggle hard to speak
Stifled by fits of tears, of helpless rage
Weathers of many seasons laid this flock
Low to the field, in the cold mists of age

Caller with flowers, hear the murmur, the whisper
In frail leaves still golden, still alive
Many skills and loves in humble cells
Unreachable sweetness in the winter hive

*Bethia Bell, Putney*

# A MOTHER'S DAY

Up at six, now let's see
Wake the children it's time to be
Getting ready for school till three
What's the day got in store for me
The washing, cleaning and beds to strip
Then another shopping trip
Gather articles in a bin sack
Put it out quick, the dustman's back
I'll make sure he doesn't lose half down the track
Or it's more sweeping up another sack
Clean up dishes, washing machine on
Make the beds, oops, it's time I was gone
Back home quick, put dinner on
Load the drier, hoover the floor
Oh, what's that, a knock on the door
Children home time to rest and be at ease
Washing up done, watch them undress for bed
Time for me to rest my weary head
What's tomorrow hold for me
The same old thing round till tea

*D Blackboro, Grays*

**Douglas Blackboro** started writing 15 years ago after a nervous breakdown. "I found that words came easily," he explained. "My work is influenced by people and their ways and also everyday events and I would like to remembered as a caring person." Aged 48 he works as a cabinet maker, carpenter and joiner and his ambition is to see his four children grow up. "I've written about 50 poems but this is the first time I have had one published," he said. He has also written several short stories.

## MUM

I wish God would have let
You stay, a little longer by my side
To let you see who I've become
How I have changed from child
To mum

*J Noll, Eastbourne*

## GENTLE FATHER

Gentle father, lord of all
On land and sea and sky
Made the creatures great and small
And taught the birds to fly
Built the mighty mountain tall
And covered it with snow
Came to make the waterfall
And tides that ebb and flow
Taught the birds to sing their tunes
And painted rainbows bright
Came to show the stars and moon
The way to light the night
Came to make the sky above
And formed the deep blue sea
Thank you for all those I love
And all you do for me
Keep me near and in your care
And show me wrong from right
And come to hear the children's prayer
I say to you tonight

*Keith Lewis, Greenford*

THE END OF A CENTURY

File
Homelessness, unemployment, poverty, neglect

Exit
War, depression, technology, disaster

Are you sure you want to exit this windows session?
Yes

*Suzanne Mudd, Grays*

SOCIETY

Blame government and teachers, the council if you like
Opposition party or wrong bill of rights
When what matters does not work as it should
Blame something or someone, they were no good
Doctors, lawyers, religion, the media too
Yes, blame the lot, any or all will do

Stop looking outside to solve your woes
Inside has the answer to make all problems go
Prevention is better than cure, listen to your own soul
Take responsibility not half, but whole

Society is made from me and you
All kinds of people what are you going to do?
Continue to blame others just pass the buck
Stop pointing the finger make your own luck

Society is made from you and me
All of us must accept responsibility

*Jenefer Adams, Southall*

MY HERO

I was hoping for some quality
Communication, I said
Is that Mercury or BT?
Joked he
Neither, just you and me

He sat on the other settee
Holding up in front of him
An upright wooden chair
Which he twirled
And jabbed as if to scare
A lion back to its lair.
Peering through the bars
His body language
Spoke loud and clear

Last night I dreamed
Of a strong kind of hero
Who protected me.
It wasn't he

*Lindsay Chi, Brighton*

**Lindsay Chi** said: "My first poem, written in my teens, is
sadly lost, but I do have nearly one hundred spanning 20
years. Four have been published in anthologies by Poetry
Now and Anchor Books. Once a solitary activity, I am now
able to share my writing with other women through a nur-
turing group at Brighton Women's Centre. My work as a
health visitor is challenging. My partner is a fellow Aries.
We both married twice and have grown-up children. I
dream of early retirement in the Canary Islands, writing in
a villa with sea and mountain views and a swimming
pool..."

# THE GLINT OF THE SPITFIRE

The glint of the spitfire as it flies by the sun
Of a time immemorial we all fought as one
The dark days of war saw their light in the sky
The crackle and rattle of the battle on high
As they fought for the lives of the people next door
There were those on the ground who questioned what for?
The roar of the engine at last now is stilled
The tears are all shed for those that were killed
The hangers are gone nothing left of their deeds
The fate of an airfield now covered in weeds

*Neville Withers, Acton*

Dedicated to 'The Few' and ground crews who made it possible.

# MY LOVE IS STRONG

My love is strong and knows no bounds
I love you deeply my rose coloured clown
Though you taunt me and tease me
As only you I allow
Where are you my sweet as I think
Of you now

Each moment, each hour, each day
That goes by
Is spent thinking and dreaming
And wondering why
My heart sings at the thought
Of your tender kiss
Loving you darling
Is eternal bliss

*Paula Fanthorpe, Lewes*

# SADNESS

Is it just I who seeks to find
The only way to possibly be kind
Is it not wrong to turn away
From a lonely child, or an animal stray

A feeling of sadness I sometimes feel
When I am ignored as I plead my will
If knowing the difference from wrong and right
Why do people make the world a horrible sight

The start of a discussion
The ending of war
The homeless, the starving
Does it have to go on anymore

When I am let down by people I know
Or missing a person that had to go
I ask myself what I did wrong
A tear trickles down my face, no shoulder to cry on

My confusion takes me to a threatened country at war
My own pain and anger has stopped once more
I forget my broken heart and the pointless shout of a voice
My feelings and heart go out to those who don't have a choice

*Corinna Louise Collins, Grays*

"I am 19-years-old and I am a qualified Nursery Nurse. 'Sadness' is my first atempt of serious poetry, expressing how I feel," said **Corinna Collins**. "Thanks to my parents I have travelled and seen many countries, from a young age, including Vietnam, Nepal and Thailand, where my brother Wayne currently lives. This has opened my mind and influenced me. In the near future, I plan to work abroad and do performing arts. I love the outdoor world and my favourite hobby is horse-riding. I enjoy going out with my friends and like to meet new people. I have had a happy upbringing, surrounded by my family and many animals."

# OH! TO BE IN EASTBOURNE

Oh woe, to be in Eastbourne
Now that summer's here
The handkerchief-on-head brigade
Are paddling by the pier
Perspiring, ice-cream munching
Rows of oiled and frying flab
Adorn the sweating beaches
Like dead codfish on a slab

Oh joy, to be in Eastbourne
Now summer's on the wane
Tomato-tinted tourists
Pack coach and car and train
With brimming bags of Soltan
Souvenirs and shells and pics
Our trippers, students, everyone
Is heading for the sticks

Please pardon this poor cynic
Only trying to be funny
Return next year, dear each and all
And bring your lovely money

*Angie Creed, Eastbourne*

# AUTUMN

The leaves are turning on the bough and the nights are
drawing in
Radiant days are cooling down and rooks have ceased their
din
The autumn colours soon will glow with many a varied hue
And skies will fade to winter grey, goodbye to summers
blue

The golden sheaves are gathered, the apples rosy red
The church its harvest home has held and prayers of
thanks been said
The seasons come, the seasons go, and we are ever blessed
With all the earth's rich bounty, ensured at God's behest

The great creator's talents are manifold to see
And we his humble children should always grateful be
Dear Lord of field and hedgerow, of summer sun and rain
Look to our needs and nurture us, till springtime comes
again

*Marion P Webb, Bromley*

"Having spent my entire working life in various branches of
the nursing profession, I now have time in retirement to
indulge in my hobby of verse," explained **Marion Webb**.
"This started at the early age of ten, sustained me through
wartime and throughout my career. Happily many of my
efforts have been published, so I hope they have given plea-
sure to others."

# THE POET'S DAWN

Come early by the dawn
And seize the tempting gate
Come willing heart, recall the dimming echo
And play upon the dream
That sped you through the night
Till borrowed light - in sight of dawn

Hear the trees in muddled song
Tease the fauna, gentle wake
Embrace your smile on natures eyes
Let her charm seduce your arm
The warming light delights the hand
A blushing hand, denuding dawn

Blushing words, just kissing dawn
Oh so silent.....painted dawn
The poet breathes bewitched, content
And fair is born the pristine morn
Come sir melt in haste
And meet its glowing wake
Contrary to the dawn

*Dudley Crundall, Romney Marsh*

## IMMACULATE PERCEPTION

When autumn's leaves are softly shed
When winter's silk is laid
The spring-time sun
And summer fun
Remove our masquerade

The melody of new-born birds
The tincture in the tree
Enjoying days
Of art displays
In nature for all to see

The radiance of the golden glow
Like paint so bright and mild
The endless weeks
And hide-and-seeks
So loved by every child

But now the laughter is in the mist
The body I that wear
Can not rejoice
In youthful voice
I'm here but also there

*Bradley Jacob, Newport*

**Bradley Jacobs** told us: "I've always thought that if people enjoy reading my work as much as I delight in writing it, then the aim of my poetry is truly fulfilled. Even though I may have only experienced a mere 18 years in this world, my feelings about love, death and the development of the human being - both body and soul - are openly conveyed through my work. I would describe my style as 'easily accessible' to the reader, yet 'ultimately personal' to not just myself, but also to the reader themselves. Besides poetry I like to socialise and I have ambitions to travel."

IF ONLY

If only my little girl could talk
If only my little girl could walk
If only my little girl could run
And have fun in the summer sun
If only my little girl could see
If only, that is my one plea
If only she could say, "I have a pain in my tummy"
If only say, "I love you Mummy"

*Reigna Mitchell, Peacehaven*

This poem is dedicated to a brave little girl, 11-year-old
Hoi-Yee Tang, who has severe celebral palsy.

**Reigna Mitchell** writes poetry between work on a novel
about a large family at the early part of the century. "I'm
hoping to finish the book and have it published," she said.
Born in Redhill, Surrey she is married to Arthur and has
five children and 15 grandchildren, plus two cats. Aged 56,
she works as a voluntary carer. "I have always liked to
write but having five children, spare time was at a premi-
um," she explained. "I started going to creative writing
classes at the start of 1998 and my work is mostly influ-
enced by wildlife and the South Downs."

# THE WIND

Blowing and roaring through the sky
I will worry you to sleep

I will madly roar and blow

Blowing and roaring through the sky
I will scatter the trees

I will madly roar and blow

Blowing and roaring through the sky
I will soar through the plain green fields

I will madly roar and blow

Blowing and roaring through the sky
So stormy I am

I will madly roar and blow

Blowing and roaring through the sky
Rushing and bowing the trees across fields

Then softly, I die down to a whisper

*Katherine Higham, Acton*

A pupil at St Peter's C of E Primary School in Hammersmith, London W6, **Katherine Higham** was ten-years-old when she wrote this poem. She enjoys reading poetry and, like most children, had written the occasional poem of her own. However, it was only during an English lesson - while discussing different techniques used in poetry - that she became aware of the strength of a repeating line or phrase (used with dramatic effect in "The Wind"). Now 11 and looking forward to starting secondary school in September, Katie hopes to continue her search for the illusive "Laureate"!

## QUESTIONS

Could nature ever better
The beauty that is you?
Could God above alone create
Such loveliness to view?
Could artists ever capture
Your smouldering, sensuous looks?
Could authors ever find the words
To describe you in their books?
Could lovers ever witness
The magic of your charms?
Could sunlight ever hope to match
The warmth found in your arms?
Could wizards manufacture
The spell you hold me by?
Could diamonds ever re-create
The sparkle in your eye?
Could philosophers unravel
The mysteries that you hide?
Could I ever love another?
I couldn't if I tried

*Robbie Pettitt, Rochford*

# THE TENDER TRAP

A wondrous smile that made you melt
His eyes so full of fun
Too long, it seemed, before I felt
That he must be the one

He picked me up when life had knocked me down
His warmth and kindness always did abound
He managed to remove my furrowed frown
As joyous laughter became our sound

He taught me everything I know
About so many things
How you've always got to go, go, go
And not wait in the wings

I grew to love him, oh so much
His wit beyond compare
His hands that had the gentlest touch
Time so precious did we share

But then it all did fall apart
As he became so ill
And I was left - a shattered heart
Love lost - forever still

*Jill N Ronald, Haywards Heath*

Dedicated in ever loving memory of Girocco from his mistral.

## SWEETHEART'S SONG

I'll twine white violets and myrtle green
Narcissis, tulips, where the grass is seen
Sweet crocus and hyacinth blue
To show you that my love is true

To deck my darling's tresses sweet
With your two lovely little feet
Red rosy cheeks, soft scented breast
Where in the eyes and nose do nest
Sweet lips that perfect pleasure bring
Sing me your love sweetheart please sing
And make me feel just like a king

I have no one to love me now
No dear hands to touch my brow
Those loving hands to clasp into mine

That made us close to love divine
I miss those tears you shed for me
The love in your eyes I can clearly see
Your lovely hair so golden and fair
I knew that always you would be there

*F C V Bathurst, West Ealing*

WHITSTABLE

The horned vikings called it Witanstaple
Village of wise men and market place
Ruler Agricola, praised it for its natives
Oysters, pride of every Roman's table

Tucked into a bay, shingle edged
Its fishermen's cottages gable roofed
Crooked with age, white wood painted
Upturned boats stand hidden in sand and sedge

Ebb tide and the puddled, glistening mud flats
Lie virgin, seaweed streaked, pod and wrack
The cockle spits and a curious bird
Head cocked, searches beneath the soft fronded mat

Beach huts, gaily painted, guard the shore
Nearby small boats in a tangle of tall masts
Stand stark in the strange beauty of the place
Washed in a blood red sunset welcoming nights closing
door

*Joan Sheppard, Whitstable*

# THE MIRROR

These eyes of mine I behold
Seeking in their depths
For reasons to be told
Of how and why I feel this way
Unresolved questions every day

These eyes of mine I behold
Filled with glistening tears
I'm unable to withhold
Pretty face no longer do I see
Sheer sadness staring straight back at me

These eyes of mine I behold
Lost in the madness of my mind
Empty and seemingly, oh so cold
He's reached me after all these years
Ominously neglectful of my fears

These eyes of mine I behold
Now, no longer speak to me
Twas years since they were so bold
Lost forever in the vortex of my mind
Where there's him and me, two of a kind

*B J Polhill, Lindfield*

**Brenda Polhill**, author of "The Mirror" has been writing verse for just 18 months and is influenced tremendously by her volatile moods. She finally found the inspiration she needed when she took English classes at her local college in Holywords Heath, where her tutor gave her the encouragement she had been seeking. Her admiration for all artists of creativity is immense and her greatest wish would be to leave at least one piece of her work behind for others to take pleasure in. Brenda is married with one daughter. She hopes to eventually publish a collection of her poems.

# HE WASN'T INTENDING TO GRUNT

She'd been leaning sideways
Ahead of him on the second set
Of escalators, her Lorna Doone hair
Caped across the briefest of tops
With sunned thighs stretched
From the kind of skirt
We'd all have panted after
Thirty years ago.

Wedged between cases, he'd tired
Of inventing reasons to fiddle
With his watch, or of trying
To take an interest in advertisements.
So, before she flipped her shades
To swivel him one of her most
Derisory glances, why didn't she look?
He wore his love on his left-hand finger:
He had three daughters;
He had white hair;
He was invisible.
Hadn't she noticed?

*David Goodall, Hailsham*

**David Goodall** has included "He Wasn't Intending to Grunt" in
his sequence of poems called "Holding Hands with Prufrock" ISBN
1 900 447 177, obtainable from 64, Hawkswood Drive, Hailsham,
East Sussex BN27 1UR  for £2.50 including postage. Featured in
Poetry Nottingham, published in some 30 small press magazines
and broadcast on radio and TV, David is available for
readings/talks: contact at address above.

PEACE AND LIGHT

From beginning to end we faced
The fear, from light to dark we
Circled here, from good to bad we
Laughed we cried, from cold winter
Nights outside, to golden beaches
Moons and tides
From people to places, to lovers
And faces, love scenes from Utopia
A unity of seeds, of nurtured
Earthlings in a heavenly breeze

From nothing to everything and
Back again, from full and pure to
Empty and thin
I know you're listening, I can hear
Your mind
Are you scared
Where do we go from here?

Peace and light a unity from within

*Richard Barnes, Ashford*

## MY SISTER BARBARA

Dear sister Barbara
Spain she lives
Arrivals are so lovely
Beautifully be-hatted
Lovely roses on her hat
Like the breath of spring she brings
Gay are the dresses she wears
Butterflies fly around her to catch her lovely scent

Love - she gives so freely
Understanding is one of her arts
Tenderness is her treasure
She has to help all who cross her path

Happiness she gives
Like stars shining brightly all the time
As pretty as a picture is Barbara
Leonora is her second name
Graceful and elegant is she

May she be happy in her life
As she gives so much to others
Dear sister Barbara
God bless you in life

*Ann Sheridan, Hanwell*

Just six lines of poetry started the writing career of **Ann Sheridan**. "When I was 18 I wrote a few lines and a teacher liked my work and encouraged me," she explained. "My work is influenced by a relative - Richard Brinsley Sheridan." Now aged 61, Ann is a retired civil servant who enjoys books, antiques and writing. She has written a book and also 200 poems but this is the first poem which she has had published. "The person I would most like to meet is Prince Charles because he is such a deep thinker," she said.

I REMEMBER

I remember the brickfield pond
Where we children used to play
And old Phil Jenner moulding the bricks
From the good old Sussex clay

And the brick kilns glowing red at night
Drying the bricks he made
The council houses are standing now
On the land where we children played

And over the moor (as we called it then)
Where St Wilfrids school is today
There once was a fair with a jungle ride
Where we children used to play

*O Hilton, Haywards Heath*

LIFE

You have to creep before you crawl
And crawl before you walk
You have to breathe before you cry
And cry before you talk
You have to kneel before you stand
And stand before you run
And with the help of God
You'll be a man, my son

*E M Stevens, Canvey Island*

## THE FOUR SEASONS

It's sad to see the fallen leaves rotting on the ground
But that is natures way of saying autumn has come round
With summertime behind us, and all her blossoms gone
We look ahead to winter, and hope it won't stay long
T'is then we think of Christmas with its glory and good
cheer
And we celebrate the Saviours birth, for He is held so dear
Next we have the thought of spring with all new life appear-
ing
The leafy trees, the bluebell woods, the song birds we'll be
hearing
The temperature is rising, the sun is in full view
We are blessed with all four seasons which bring us some-
thing new
We marvel at creation, God must have had good reason
For all the changes that he made to each and every season

*Sylvia Hills, Epsom*

## AUTUMN SHOPPING

Howling winds assail the trees
The roads awash with rain
Oil slicks floating as it gushes
On towards the drain

Cars constantly arriving
And parking in a bay
Disgorging eager shoppers
Equipped to join the fray

The giant dome absorbs them all
And spins them round inside
Then spews them out with goods piled high
Against the inward tide

The loaded cars leave slowly
Suspension hanging low
The cars of shoppers left inside
Stand row on row on row

*Michael Morton, Faversham*

HOTEL HEAVEN

It's been here for centuries, this hotel that no one leaves
It's miles above sea level, so the guests can barely breathe
The room service is terrible, as the staff are very old
But no one dares to go outside, "You'll burn your face",
they're told
Winter is the busiest season, icy roads provide demand
You'll wait for years to sign your name, for this divine
remand
One monolingual receptionist, results in lengthy queues
The singles are full, you'll have to share
With who you cannot choose
The entertainment's limited, some pot plants and a church
The all-sky view will never change, despite your daily
search
Downstairs there is a party, but you're denied this endless
rave
Every Sunday you prayed to come here, you wanted to be
saved

*Sarah Thurling, Epsom*

This poem is dedicated to Matt McDonald, my partner and
best friend. Thanks for everything, all my love, Sarah.

# THE BOX

Nice things happened when the TV broke
My husband moved, he even spoke
I remembered his voice from long ago
When all we had was the radio
He rose from his chair and then he said
"I might as well go to bed"

*G Barton, Wimbledon Common*

# WHISTLER MOUNTAIN

I gaze in awe at Whistler Mountain
Whose peaks are richly coned with snow
Where pine trees green in countless thousands
Embrace the mountain row on row

The winding roads to Whistler Mountain
Rough-hewn through rock and roots of pine
Expose coarse scars of spoliation
By man's keen urge to redesign

The grizzly bear here wanders freely
And birds of every size and hue
Know secret lairs and concealed dwellings
Where furtive creatures hide from view

I stand beneath great Whistler Mountain
Whose white clad peaks near scrape the sky
I think of life, of age and wonder
Why we, not mountains, have to die

*Patrick Redmond, Richmond*

## DESOLATE

A desolate room
No decoration, no furniture
No lights, no windows
No heating for comfort
No door for people to enter
Just a desolate room
A room by itself
In a desolate land

*Grace Drewell, West Wickham*

## MY MUSICAL HERO

On September the seventh in the year of sixty six
This miracle of music was born of hits
At the age of five on a toy violin
A five dollar prize was where it began

From fifty eight to fifty nine he wrote his own words
Along with the Crickets, who showed lots of nerve
Early hits were very hard work
All over the world his music was heard

In the freezing weather of fifty nine
On the third of February all went quiet
His plane had crashed near Mason city
Talented Buddy no longer with us

A legend of music in his time
Buddy wrote music, superb, sublime
That'll be the Day was his greatest hit
In the year of the nineties, he's very much missed

*Patricia Smith, Ashford*

A FAR CRY

It's a far cry
From the back to the front of the queue

It's a far cry
From the bottom to the top of the pile
Where you can just make out the high-ups smile

It's a far cry
From here to the other side of the tracks
Where the only sound coming back
Is of the glitterati saying, "Keep down, shaddup"

It's a far cry

It's a far cry

It's a far cry

*Michael Byrne, Folkestone*

**Michael Byrne** started writing poetry at the age of 13 after his experiences in a social services home. "It was a kind of self therapy," he said. "My work is influenced by man's follies and I would like to be remembered as the person who showed humanity its reflection in the mirror of life." Michael is 39-years-old, works in PR and has two daughters. He has written many poems and had several of them published. He is also the author of "The Nervous Revolution" ISBN 1-902077-00-8. His hobbies include reading, writing, walking and Earth sciences.

## THE WALK

Mud from the Stour stains
Sticking, clogging and dragging down
Aches and longing
Another obstacle and spilling more
Than you can swill
On and smoking another, falling still
Falling till the mud drags
you down
And knees crack before you turn for home

*Tim Bratton, Ashford*


## THEY PLAYED TOY SOLDIERS

I saw the boy who hid beneath the fire
And I felt no incline to take his hand
For frolicked in his eye the raw desire
To bury fellow men beneath the sand
They landed, sweat and soiled, toy soldiers stood
To clasp the metal deep within their hearts
Where cherished moments and sweethearts once could
Bring hope and calm when all else good departs
They played toy soldiers running through the sea
A silent mirror shattered by the gun
Adrenaline was life's last ecstasy
In duty fell, the game had lost its fun
From innocence there grew a sickly strife
This man would give his country for his life

*Rosalind Wright, Burgess Hill*

## 55

I can't believe I'm 55
Here I am still alive
Some teeth have gone, the eyes are poor
Dance till dawn I can no more
I work all day and sleep all night
The back is stiff, but health's all right
My middle thickens day by day
This extra weight won't stay away
Back to the gym, I'll fight this fat
Old age - rubbish, I can't have that

*Eunice Abbott, Richmond*

Born in Cardiff, **Eunice Abbott** started writing poetry two
years ago after the death of a special friend "Soon after-
wards my brother, who wrote poetry, also died," said
Eunice. "After that I just kept writing. It was as though it
was passed on to me through him." Aged 58, she is a beau-
ty therapist and has fulfilled her ambitions to have her own
beauty salon plus a wonderful family and children. She is
married to Mike and has two children Lucy (23) an actress
and Tom (19), a student. She has had several poems pub-
lished in local magazines and has also had her history of
the beauty business printed. Her hobbies include charity
and Rotary work plus researching her family history.

# TRUE FRIENDS

To go to the shops,
To paint the town red.
To not have to worry,
About the price of bread.

To walk the streets at night,
And not to be frightened to go out.
To feel a sense of inner peace,
And happy without doubt.

To take new steps
And make many friends.
And to feel with them,
All my problems end.

Because I know they care
Through good and troubled times,
I know they will always be there.

*Gillian Grainger, West Hoathly*

"I started writing poetry in 1996 and am influenced by many things, especially the beauty of the world around me," said **Gillian Grainger**, author of "True Friends". Aged 45 she is a school cleaner and her main hobby is writing poetry although she has other ambitions, as she explained: "I would love to do some work as a TV extra and also travel to visit countries." She is married to Tony and has two sons David and Raymond, plus a pet dog, Sam. "I would like to be remembered as someone who cares about other people and I like to be surrounded by my family and friends," she said. Her biggest fantasy is to go on a cruise to visit relatives she hasn't seen for many years.

# YE OLD CANVEY ISLAND

Zwygent Nacht heilig Nacht
All is bright, all is calm
From shepherd to farm we can
Now lift an arm

All is one with the natures
Of the world, from east and west
Or from the four corners his
Lips curled

The wind bloweth over many
From capitals of foreign parts
And the mainland like an egg
Timer that breathes life
With the gushing of the sand

Upon the face and from the sight
Of the magic eye
For three hundred years long
Its voice had a song from King
To a pirate that led the torch that
Burneth around the wheel turneth

*Susan White, Canvey Island*

Born and brought up in Canvey Island, **Susan White** is a
bookshop owner who has already had four of her poems
published. She has also written "A History of Canvey Island
- Five Generations" available from - The Bookshop, 27b
High Street, Canvey Island, Essex at £9.99. "I started writing during my teens and my other hobbies are reading,
swimming and history," she said. She was educated at
Timberlog School in Basildon, Grays Technical College and
Charlotte Mason Teacher Training College and taught in
schools in Luton and Stanford-Le-Hope.

TO A STRANGER

Your hair is a glistening gold with a hint of red
It cascades over your shoulders as you turn your head
It's soft and shiny and smells of perfume
And everyone glances as you enter the room
When you walk it seems to waltz on its own
And bounce as if it needs to be shown
As a seeker of beauty could I admire your hair?
Could I take you to dinner in Brighton somewhere?
And enjoy your lovely, long, golden, red hair
I'm not young, not rich, not handsome, not charming
Would there be any harm in our meeting?

*Doug Streeter, Brighton*

**Doug Streeter**, author of "To a Stranger" has been "in print" since he was 16-years-old before the war when he was a "copy boy" with a London publishers. "After war service I found myself in Fleet Street but not as a journalist and was there for 25 years. However I wrote a weekly column in a local newspaper. Indeed I still do," said Doug. This is his only poem and was inspired, written and given to a stranger on the Dieppe ferry. "Well, the trip does take four hours and she was sitting right opposite me," added Doug.

# THE WAITING ROOM

With heavy heart I ventured south
To Hythe to be exact
A visit to my dentist
I hope he won't extract

I feel just like a child of four
At his first days school
Better pull myself together
Better keep my cool

I know he wants to hurt me
He'll prod and probe around
He'll pull and scrape and fill and drill
God, I hate that sound

I wish there was another way
I wish this was another day
My palms are sweating now, my heart is doing backflips
"Could someone wipe my brow?"

The sweat is running in my eyes
My dentist thinks it's tears
"Come now sir, don't cry", he says
And tries to calm my fears

It's much too late, I'm all worked up
I hope it's over soon
I think I could have been quite brave
Had I left the waiting room

*P Bridgeman, Ashford*

## SUMMER THOUGHTS

When the air is warm and clear
When the evening is drawing near
And a bird begins to sing
Ah, that is what I love to hear
More than anything

It is the sweetness of the sound
That pleases so, joy has no bound
As when a gift with love is brought
Sent then my feelings high, profound
And I beneath am stilled in thought

And think on joy, and think on grace
The two at zenith interlace
Perfection ever was at one
With beauty in a happy place
Of evening air and late, late sun

*Mary Powell, Brighton*

Born in London, **Mary Powell** inherited her interest in poetry and art from her parents and was first published in her school magazine as a youngster. "My work is influenced by my feelings and joy at regaining my sight and some of my health," she said. "I would describe my style as formal for serious poetry but free-style for humorous verse." Aged 80, she is retired and her ambition is to continue to enjoy and appreciate life. "I have never wished to be anyone other than myself and am content with all the friends I have. I am very lucky to have so many," she said. She has written a biography of her father in collaboration with the late Richard Findlater of the Observer and the book, published in 1979. "Little Tich - Giant of the Music Hall", is available in libraries - ISBN 0241101743.

# ROADWORKS

"We apologise for any inconvenience
Essential works are being undertaken
The work will last for six weeks
Work will commence on Monday 22nd June"

Men arrive with picks, shovels, a convenience
Traffic lights, cones, barriers, neighbours awaken
To compression drills, I had reported water leaks
in March.
"We will attend to the matter very soon"

Warm work and good weather encourage men
To bare torsos and legs of mid oak colour
A particularly good looking guy poses for the girls
In the office across the way The Fox and Hounds

Becomes the meeting place for them all, landlord Len
Looks very cheerful, his wife Sal, adores odour
Of manly sweat, with them laughs, tossing her curls
And encouraging them to spend more, a trading boom

"Road clear, sorry for any inconvenience"
Gloria and Sylvia the morning after pill have taken
The good looking guy - a casual - new work seeks
The girls dream of him bathed in light of a full moon

*Andrew P F Duncan, Portslade*

GROWING UP

Why do I have to take a bath
Share my toys, walk on the path
Mum won't let me stay up late
Or keep worms for fishing bait

I'd take apart my electric train
(I'm sure I could put it together again)
My room could be a work of art
If only mum would let me start

Do I have to eat up all my greens
Throw away my holey jeans
Be nice and kiss my Aunty May
(It's not even my birthday)

I don't want to go to school
I'd rather catch tadpoles in the pool
I'll go and call for my best mate
It's a hard life being only eight

*Bronwyn Dunnett, Clacton-On-Sea*

BIT BY BIT

When I was born I'm sure I came with all the parts I needed
But to keep them all in working nick I've simply not succeeded

The doctor pointed at my tum - "That birthmark looks suspicious"
They took it off when I was ten - a start not so auspicious

A pair of dodgy tonsils were the next for them to get
I suppose they took my adenoids just to complete the set

When in my middle years I knew my family was completed
By a womb and both my ovaries the inventory depleted

But on the subject of my teeth - what more is there to say?
A lot have gone before me - they've already passed away

I must tell all those who know me to enjoy me while they can
I'm returning to the maker on God's own instalment plan

*Stella Backham, Wickford*

BRAVEHEART

Hope just a word, out served its purpose
Despair now used - reality strikes
Years of fighting to no avail
Why can't life be a fairytale?

So tough in fight, brave in defeat
The trying is over - boy, did he try
Another victim to the big C assassin
My daddy, my father, my next of kin

Just a matter of time - be ready, I'm told
Make comfortable, he sleeps - I hold his hand
Only a young man, so full of life
I imagine - prepare for the tears and strife

My mother, my brothers all whom concerned
How will they cope and me - I'm scared
I want to be the pillar of strength, yes I
To make my father proud when he looks from the sky

Inevitability draws near, I know in my heart
I want to tell dad everything but where do I start
He will never be forgotten that big man so tall
The gentle giant, the bravest of all

*Daniel Riggs, Basildon*

Dedicated to my father Clifford Riggs "Braveheart" who never gave
up fighting and taught us all the meaning of life.

# HALCYON DAYS

To lie in a field - wherein daisies abound
Feel the sun on your face - and the air all around
Is scented and soft as thistledown
To walk down the lane where blossoming trees
Are weighted with sweetness inviting the bees
To alight and drink their fill
To stroll by the lake - silvered moon above
Where the nightingale pours out his song of love
For all the world to hear
To sit on a rock gazing out to sea
And see the gulls flying wild and free
The water crystal clear
To see rolling hills with misty shrouds
Of purple light that meet the clouds
And so become as one
Always treasure these days within your heart
For throughout life they will impart
A kind of benediction

*Irene Bishop, Ashford*

# THE BLACKMAN

The blackman stood in the dark of the night
His three piece suit a glimmering white
Standing as still as a man could be
Could it be he was watching me
I had to walk and pass him by
Only the moon lit up the sky
I passed him by in terrible fear
He said nothing but shed a tear
I began to feel really shy
Then he disappeared in the blink of an eye

*Tracy Verrall, Brighton*

**Tracy Verrall**, author of "The Blackman" said: "I have been writing verse for 16 years. I was encouraged to write about memories of my awful childhood, in the hope that people would understand and help me. I found it difficult to talk about. I wrote it in verse and it helped, then I began to write about other subjects. I am married to Stephen and we have three children. We enjoy walking, cycling and board games. I've also written my life story. If anyone would like to see more of my work, please write to: 170 Heath Hill Avenue, Brighton BN2 4LS."

# YEAH, WHATEVER

We used to go walking on the moor
Stumbling around in the dark
We'd worship at the temple with words idly swapped
And laugh into the night air
She talked of flowers and the change they could bring
She talked of India and sitting naked in mango trees
I tried to be there but couldn't move
She talked of having babies but not just yet
She talked of him
And I may have mentioned her

We used to go walking on the moor
Striding around in the sun
It was easier and harder being able to see
But it was never just the two of us
The sky was blue and the air was beautiful
As we matched our steps and exchanged our histories
More complete opposites surely impossible to find
But you know what they say
She said she missed him but it was nice to be alone
I said, "Yes, it's nice to be alone"

*Graeme Allan, Brighton*

## LAZY BONES

I'm safe indoors the fire glows
I feel its warmth around my toes
I'm in a very lazy mood
But guess it's 'cos I'm full of food

The sun comes out and puts on show
My cobwebs and they're all aglow
They really are so very pretty
To dust them off would be a pity

I'll just sit here and rest and dream
Enjoying winter's cosy scene
Now everything can rest a while
Before spring comes with happy smile

I'll sit around and stroke the cat
Both he and I are fond of that
A jigsaw puzzle I might try
Providing there's not too much sky

A crossword puzzle could be fun
But so is tea and toasted bun
I don't find winter dull or grey
I just enjoy each lazy day

*Diane Jones, Brighton*

Dedicated to my cat Thomas who taught me the art of relaxation.

**Diane Jones**, author of "Lazy Bones" has been writing poetry since she was a child. Her poems reflect the lighter side of life. She has had much of her work published in magazines and newspapers and is currently working on her own book of comic verse, which she hopes to get published in the future. Now retired, she said. "Much of my inspiration came from working in a toyshop. Children say the funniest things!" Diane is married and enjoys working on her computer in the winter and going on walks in the summer.

TWO OF FIVE

The purple haze has passed
Through the contemporary
To the history
Leaving contentment
To fill the void
That shook foundations

*Matt Rowley, Eastbourne*

**Matt Rowley**, author of "Two of Five", wrote a small collection of poems whilst living in Australia with his girlfriend, Nyomi. "I like to write poems spontaneously, when the moment or the state of mind needs to be remembered," he explained. "This poem is especially important to me as it was written when my sense of smell and taste came back after a year, following an accident, hence the title, meaning the return of two of the five senses." Author also of a short story called "Nexus Rage", Matt is a Website Architect. Contact can be made through Independent Webrications unLtd at http:www.overflow.demon.co.uk/.

IN THE SUN

In the sun I see your smile
In the rain I see your pale blue eyes
Across the golden blanket fields
I see your flowing long blonde hair
Look up at the soft clouds
Your lips breathe warm air
Beauty all around
I can see you everywhere
In my alphabet soup
I see the name Jantine written there
Close my eyes, I think of you
You mean so much to me
Without you, my world would
Simply be bare

*Matthew Hawkins, Crawley*

ESSEX COUNTY

This Essex is a lovely part of England, quite unique
It offers joy to everyone no matter what we seek
Old churches stand, reminders of its long history
Through all the years they've witnessed
Peace and wars and mystery

Seaside towns so modern, reached at end of line
Villages so peaceful going back in time
Little streams meander lazily along
Heaven for the fishermen softly humming song

Bustling towns now thriving with everything we need
Farmers on their acres, busy sowing seed
Each compliments the other, has to play its part
In making Essex county the place dear to our heart

*Rose L Pearce, Westcliff-On-Sea*

## GIVE AND TAKE

Cars fly by
Children playing
People rushing, pushing
Babies cry
Shoppers, boppers
Teeny poppers
Looking for a special tie

Excuse me
Thank you
How are you?
Nice to see you
These words you hardly hear

A little bit if giving
Can mean an awful lot
It can make life worth living
When someone may think it's not

*E M Woodford, Worthing*

I dedicate my love to my family, mum and dad, my daughter Amanda, my son Jason and my grandchildren especially my "Dave".

Born in Canada, **Elizabeth Woodford** started writing 12 years ago after having an emergency operation and spending several weeks in hospital. "My work is influenced by life around me, my feelings and my family and I would describe my style as open, based on my observations of life," she said. "I would like to be remembered as a very proud mother of two wonderful children and my wonderful grandchildren." Her ambition is to see her son collect an oscar for a film he has written. She is married to David and her hobbies include painting in oils, sewing, and, of course writing poetry. She has written short stories and many poems but this is the first time she has been published.

AH, LOVE

Ah, love
Quicksilver friend
Mercurial mentor of my soul
How constant are your afflictions
How spartan the code of your school
How fleeting your momentary affection
How bruised and beaten this dunce of a fool

*Peter Bauer, Brighton*


**Peter Bauer** is in fact long-time husband to Mary, with grown-up children Sarah and Nic. Navel gazing is never fun but it can be informative, even enlightening, and recently Peter has had time for reflection on life, from his mother's womb to the present and beyond. The poem "Ah, Love" is one of many written during this period. Peter has had a number of poems published in various anthologies and is looking forward to one day publishing his first collection. Anyone interested in discovering more about his work can contact him at 338 Queen's Park Road, Brighton BN2 2ZL.

## THE DAY OUT

Buckingham Palace and the Tower to see
Mum and dad, my sister and me

It is our very first time on an underground train
On the way home we want to try it again

The very steep steps that never stop moving
There is nothing like this in our village of Yalding

We arrived at the top and jumped off quick
Now to see the Queen, and have our picnic

To Buckingham Palace and the Tower we have been
Had our picnic in the park near the Queen

Mum and dad tired and feeling the strain
But my sister and I have been good
So we can have our ride on the underground train

*Frederick Seymour, Bromley Common*

# THE MIRROR

As I confront the mirror
Unsure of what I'll see
This scary old woman
Is staring straight at me
Her wrinkles are starting to appear
Her grey hairs beginning to show
She's obviously put on a lot of weight
And her mouth is drooping low
She's only just reached forty
And that's where life should start
Sitting at home on her own
While her husband's out playing darts
She gets stuck home with the kids
Who spend their life on the phone
Talking to all their friends
While she sits there alone
As I confront the mirror
Unsure of what I'll see
This scary old woman is there
No, that can't be me

*Emma Neale, Southend-On-Sea*

# THINK OF ME

When my time has come to leave this shell
That you know as your wife
Do not weep and think it's the end
We will meet in another life
Your love will always keep me alive
Just as long as you speak my name
I will always be beside you dear
In summer sunshine or winter rain
Think of me when the sun shines
Through the branches of the trees
Or when spring flowers open up
To welcome in the bees
Be it spring, summer or winter time
What ever the season be
Just close your eyes
And I will kiss your brow
But my darling, just think of me

*Jean Smith, Billericay*

# FIELD OF PARADISE

'Twas a full moon that night
A young women, fresh faced with not a care in the world
Walked across a field, abundant with scented blooms
She paused to inhale the assortment of perfumes which
filled the air
Delighting her senses from every direction
This was the paradise she sought
And she was in the midst of it
She felt a strange calm
A peace of mind she would never experience again
A breeze so gentle caressed her face
And the flowers danced in the wind
She lay on the bed of grass and gazed up at the stars
They were twinkling like millions of tiny torches
Casting light across the dark skies
If she prayed for a miracle
Then her plea had been answered
And she would cherish this time in her heart
Forever

*Helen Gust, Penge*

## SEVENTEEN BRIGHT NEW STARS

The year was 1996, the place is called Dunblane
Sixteen children, one adult, are gone, who can explain?
They never even stood a chance, they'd only come to school
Taken from the ones they loved by a twisted man so cruel

No excuse or explanation can take away the pain of
Seventeen missing people, murdered in Dunblane
Just take the time to think a while, of how it all began
A twisted mind, burning hatred, bullets and the gun

We all must voice our thoughts on this, to ensure that never
again
There never can or will be, another tragedy like Dunblane
Time may heal the memories, and soothe the jagged scars
And in the darkened velvet night are seventeen bright new stars

*G J Jenkins, Hove*

I wish to dedicate this the poem to the people of Dunblane. My
thoughts are with you.

Born in Wales **Glyn Jenkins** started writing poetry in his early
teenage years. "I discovered I could write poems about anything,"
he said. "My work is influenced by everyday situations and I
would describe my style as varied and impulsive." Aged 45, he is a
professional driver and his ambition is to be asked to write verse
or lyrics for a living. He has been married for 11 years to Margaret
and has two children. He has written hundreds of poems but this
is the first he has had published. Glyn's hobbies include travel
and writing.

## A MOMENT IN JUNE

Sitting on a seafront bench watching all the world go by
Fat folk, thin folk, short and tall, when suddenly they
caught my eye
Oblivious to the thronging crowd, one man, one woman
made their way
Along the white stoned promenade, you could not say that
they looked gay
Dreary by comparison, they looked old and drab
Short and ugly, faces lined with years of suffering lonely
hours
My interest grew as they drew near with hands entwined
and footsteps faced
They looked into each others eyes, 'twas then the miracle
took place
Their faces glowed with inner joy into a loveliness sublime
Emotions purged as I looked on, always remembered
That moment in time

*M Clifton, Eastbourne*

## THE MOMENT

Goosebumps on my body
A breeze that lingers on a rhyme
Some thunder in the distance
Two hearts that beat in time
The hand that reaches for salvation
Stray loner running in the wild
A single whisper on my pillow
Innocent laughter of a child
Every one an action
A single moment in time
A time to live that action
A time to feel that rhyme

*Rone, Ashford*

To my sons Arron and Jack and their mothers Helen and Angela. Four individuals - one inspiration.

Rone is the pen name of **Ty Germaine**. "I started writing poetry a couple of years ago to release emotions and search for an inner peace," he explained. "I would like to be remembered as a deep person and my work is influenced by a special love." Aged 35, he is a support worker and his ambition is to find contentment and be happy with himself. "The person I would most like to meet is the Dali Lama because he is such a peaceful and serene person," Explained Ty. He has written many poems but this is the first time he has had any of them published and his biggest fantasy is to have a book of his own in print. His hobbies include fitness, Taekwondo, snooker, Tai Chi, yoga, reading and writing verse.

# TIME TO SWITCH OFF

Stretched out,
The coloured beast,
Dazed, back broken,
The eyes dim,
Not dancing in the jungle,
Or self injured.
But hurt by man,
Careless in his care,
Dying on hard concrete,
Heavy,
Motionless,
The coloured stripes dull,
The large body still,
Wounded by man,
Ignorant of creatures of the wild,
Pity him before he dies,
The fine tiger,
Cruelly enclosed,
Blinded by tears
I switched off the television.

*Anna Parkhurst, Richmond*

A SENSELESS WASTE

Night time in the woodlands, as dark as ebony
Walk alone a winding path, which looms up eerily
Heightened senses now alert, each step brings something new
Shadows so mysterious, when coming into view

Every sound intensified, instincts that I thought dead
Re-awaken, born again, as through the woods I tread
A broken twig cracks like a whip, at once puts nerves on edge
The breaking of the silence tantamount to sacrilege

Soft winds whisper through the trees, dead leaves fall to the
ground
Owls hoot searching for a mate, a nigh unearthly sound
Somewhere in the undergrowth a rustle can be heard
Maybe just a change of perch, for a nervous bird

Deafened by the silence and blinded by the dark
Skin once brushed is sensitive, with mouth constantly parched
This then an experience that everyone should taste
To rediscover long, lost senses that have gone to waste

*Ken Smith, Grays*

## TRAMPS ON OUR STREETS

Drunkenly, wandering through their mind
Confused and bitter at life's divide
Depressed they feel rock bottom reside
No outlook, no future, nowhere to abide
Hopelessly drifting no help near at hand
Just roaming the highways or combing the land
What are the reasons not clear, can't explain
T'is one mighty struggle could drive one insane
Who do they turn to nobody knows
No light to their tunnel, no end to their road
Desperately hungry in body cold creeps
Alone in their misery tramps on our streets

*N Radford, Brighton*

## MY PAL

Wonderful friend I loved so dear
Now free from pain, is so very close
Life's very sad, we wonder why
But so very grateful for days gone by
The bond we had was one so rare
We always knew we both could share
The good times, bad times, the love and care
The fun we had, the walks, the games
Hurrying through the leafy lanes
I may not see you at my door
But our hearts are together ever more

*Jean Walker, Brighton*

# LOVE REMAINS

The quiet night in darkness waits
Emotions secrets to be told
The soul so steeped in sadness feels
The need its burden to unfold

How death represses life that's left
To those who find they are bereft
Of youth and love that time has swept
Aside in one sad moment passed

The spirit's dead, the soul emeshed
In sorrows dread of future days
Remorseless, empty, grief refreshed
Ever evolved in life's dark maze

But time like night helps quiet the mind
Anguish and tears are left behind
Love remains and in its wake
Acceptance joins life to remake

*Tilly Timbrell-Sturgeon, Hastings*

Dedicated to Harold Geoffrey Timbrell a gentle, loving husband for 40 years 11 days. Written in the dark hours of sleepnessless.

FRIEND

I wanted to tell you of my love
The love I felt
When I saw or thought of him
It was my reality
I needed to tell of the love
I felt
When he looked intensely at me
Major moments in my life
I believed in his
I took my heart out
And showed it to you
On extended hands
My friend
Then I watched you search
For tactful words
So tactlessly
Fulfiling dreadful fears
To let me know
Oh despair
You did not believe in me

*Julia Ziewe, Worthing*

## WOMAN I LOVE

She has the elements for her allies.
The fire of the stars
Burning in her heart.
The boundless seven oceans
Deep within her belly.
A woman so grounded
The weight of earth becomes her,
Yet she's free to fly her own sweet breath
And feel the wind upon her face.
She stands, fully clothed in her nakedness,
Open for the world to greet her
And for me to share her secrets.
And what of me?
May my words provide support,
I pray they never capture.
May my strength provide a shelter
For the sing song of our laughter.
May I lighten the load
The burden I bring,
So that one day,
I may fly upon her wings.

*iam, Brighton*

**iam** is an all round entertainer; dancer, multi-instrumentalist, comedian, actor and singer. Currently, he is concentrating on music which spans a wide variety of different styles but is centred around singing and vocal percussion. iam has two books and one CD of poetry, plus another three CD's of music, each with a particular feel. If you would like more information or copies of his other works, please write to him at: Third Floor, 87 Marine Parade, Brighton BN2 1AJ.

# THE SEA OR THE LOST HORIZON

Looking out, looking out
Gazing into the horizon
The sea and sky bonding as one into
A lost world, never ending
The waves rolling on until the end of time

Colours of the sea reflecting the rays
Of the sun, forming a piece of art

The sea merging into the sand, creeping
Sneaking up onto the world, only to
Recline back to the lost horizon

*Jasmine Bates, Folkestone*

# WHAT?

What causes so much pleasure?
Yet can cause so much pain
Your hands screaming with cold
Your eyes stinging in the rain
It's the two wheeled fun
Most boys like on sunny days
Called a motorbike

*J R Wheeler, Greatstone*

To my family and friends.

# EASTBOURNE IN WINTER

Eastbourne's winter shores are shorn
No sun creamed maidens deck the sand
Only joggers pound the early morn
And ice cream kiosks shuttered stand
Sturdy and strong the Martello towers
Face biting winds not Bonaparte's blast
Pallid are summers beds of flowers
While roller bladers flash by fast
Wooden benches see grey seas now
Carved with names of those denied
The sight, mourning mist shrouds the brow
On downs where US airmen died
And beachy heads full fatal attraction
Still draws souls driven to distraction

*L W Baker, Eastbourne*

To Dennis Hawes of Folkestone whose encouragement, and example by his own "War Poems", were an inspiration.

POPPY MAYDEW

I in a field of poppy maydew
Wheat and wondrous delight
On my own with my thoughts of life and insight
Something I felt, this such a beautiful life
Beyond what we live in there are so many things
That bring peace of mind, happiness and love
So many things taken for granted
Such beauty and richness in this
World hath been planted

*Carole Raymond, Colchester*

**Carole Raymond** started writing poetry at the tender age of
seven and her work is influenced by nature and her sur-
roundings. "I would describe my style as old English," she
said. "I would love to write a novel which became famous
and my ambition is to write and live in the countryside,
which I find very inspiring." Aged 32 she is a trainee aro-
matherapist. She has one daughter, Jodie aged five.
Carole's hobbies include music, literature and art. "Poppy
Maydew" is the first poem she has ever had published.

# THE COLD-GREY DAWN OF DAY

Deaths deadly sticks are gone away
And consequence is out of sight
Until the cold-grey dawn of day

Now limping home, Viola Gaye
All through the starry, flak-filled night
Deaths deadly sticks are gone away

A ball of flame has quit the fray
Not missed beneath the droning flight
Until the cold-grey dawn of day

Must be the coast of France we say
Then Dover cliffs in eerie light
Deaths deadly sticks are gone away

Crew ditching-drill now under weigh
No time for stomach-churning fright
Until the cold-grey dawn of day

With Skip to fly and us to pray
He'll safely land the stricken kite
Deaths deadly sticks are gone away
Until the cold-grey dawn of day

*Ron Dean, Saffron Walden*

OH DEAR  ·

Wow, that was a shock
How can one person make such a din
I've tossed and turned all night long
Arose in the morning, face like sin
It never came up, when we spoke to the vicar
My inlaws never warned me
Is there nowhere written in law
That earth shattering rumbles need sorting
I suppose now we're married
There is no escaping
I did say for better or worse
I wish I had bought that heather
This was the old gypsies curse

*Carole Fendt, Deal*

REMEMBER ME

Not many now can penetrate
And breach that veil of time
To pace that path of all our dreams
Back from this peace sublime
The thunder of the battle burst
Right through that life we had
So many young lives, cast away
So many dreams they had
The past grows dim, and memory fades
As years pass by, remember me
A dot in your life for a silent prayer
For a life I gave to eternity

Remember 11th hour, 11th day, 11th month

*Thomas Victor Healey, Wimbledon*

## OUTCRY

I agree, this will not do
It's terrible, yes, yes, I agree with you

You say that there should be a law
But what is it you want it for?

Ah, to stop the use of pesticides
You say that all the frogs have died

I'll set up a committee
That's what I'll do

We'll get a result
In a year or two...

*E Root, Colchester*

## OH NO

Oh no, I said
Oh yes, you cried
I am really hurt you know
Why you said the things you did
And why you treat me so

After all, I am human
Have feelings, can't you see?
Would you like me to treat you
The same way you treat me?

Simple words can sometimes hurt
Although not meant to be
If you knew that, why you said
All that you did to me?

*R Louis, Surrey*

## SORRY

Sorry is such a simple word
Too often used to be really heard
Yet it simply says all there is to say
It says sorry for being made this way
It apologises for causing hurt and pain
And so often says, so sorry, again
Sorry for all the things I've done wrong
Sorry for not being very strong
Sorry for being just as I am
And even more sorry if it sounds like a sham

*Carol Starkey, Southminster*

**Carol Starkey**, author of "Sorry" has been writing poetry since her childhood, although she feels that most of what she writes is so personal that publication is not appropriate. However, she hopes that "Sorry" will mean something to every reader. She is a fellow of the Institute of Legal Executives and she works in the field of Criminal Defence. She and her husband are in their late 40's and they have one grown up son, and a Lakeland terrier dog.

# MONEY ISN'T EVERYTHING

There he was on the telly
A teddy just like mine
Auctioned off at Christies
Lot one hundred and nine

Of course my bear was battered
While this had fur still plush
Mine was bald in places
And didn't need a brush

It didn't have an arm gone
Or a patch upon one eye
His sawdust wasn't leaking
He sat there smart and spry

When I saw the price he fetched
I wished I hadn't played
With my dear old teddy
The fortune I'd have made

But then I thought again about
The memories we share
Tatty, worthless maybe
But you are a much loved bear

*Geraldine Foy, Horley*

# THRENODY FOR SUSSEX

The downs, undulating like gentle hump backed whales
Our sentinels both north and south crest
The changing panorama of the countryside below
Are there still skylarks trilling the air above?
Is there yet wild thyme, trefoil, scabious to grace them?
And will sheep graze, rabbit nibble preserve them
Firm, compact, to shield the weald this place of nurture
For pasture, fruiting, woods, lakes and streaming water
As nature planned, not shamefully in time succumb to
Upland overgrowth, creeping cultivation, a lower spread of
Bricks and mortar, the ribbon thread of concrete, tarmac
The mode for heedless traffic grinding by
For I would bid our would be guardians, like the downs
Coset our Countys sculpture that it might endure
Into Century twenty one for future seekers of hillsides
Wayfarers searching the valleys winding-by ways
I may not know, for my time here is on hold
Scanning only the regions of memory recaptured

*Nerine Selwood, Haywards Heath*

TICKET TO PARADISE

If you can dream the whole day long
And fill your heart the while with song
If you can make your dreams come true
And do the things you want to do
If you can bask beneath the sun
And look on life as lots of fun
And fill each idle hour with bliss
And find the time to coo and kiss
Surely then, the only price
Is the price of a ticket to paradise?

If you can let him string along
Pretending that he must belong
So he may whisper in your ear
"Darling, must it be too long?"
If you can turn night into day
And learn to chase the blues away
If you can do just what you please
Believing money grows oN trees
Surely then, the only price
Is the price of a ticket to paradise?

*Leslie Hawkins, Ealing*

## MY VANISHED YOUTH

You sneaked away from me when I wasn't looking
You flew away silently like a bird on the wing
All at once I knew
There was something missing
And nothing would be the same again
I looked in the mirror and saw I am now
A senior citizen
My soft skin and jet black hair
Has gone, you took them away with you
When you went
Why were you in such a hurry to leave me?
You could have stayed another twenty years or more
Oh how I miss you
We had some good times
And bad
But now I know you
Are gone forever
And you are never coming back
So I say farewell to you
My vanished youth

*Barbara Geraghty, Northolt*

Born in Connemara, Western Ireland **Barbara Geraghty** started writing poetry 35 years ago. "My ancestors were traditional story tellers and I am a native Irish speaker," she explained. "Poems come naturally, often when walking and are a means of self expression. My work is influenced by growing up in Connemara surrounded by the sea, land and mountains and my style is sometimes melancholy, sometimes humorous, but always from the heart." She would like to be remembered as a mother of eight children, a grandmother of nine and an Irish poet and storyteller. Aged 76 she is widowed and has one pet - Frisky, a rabbit. She has had several poems published and has also written songs, prayers and children's stories.

# THE JOURNEY

I did not travel far, just a little way from here
No preparation necessary, all travel details clear
It was a painless journey, there was no need to pack
I left behind my problems although I did look back

It was not my decision to leave without a word
Something just came over me, or perhaps a voice I heard
I cannot send a postcard, or call you on the phone, but
Please don't fret, take my word, this is home from home

I did not travel far, just a little way out there, although
There are no route maps to explain exactly where
This really is a peaceful place, I really can't complain
But I'm sorry that my leaving has caused you so much
pain

And so tomorrow morning just look up to the sky
Watch the clouds go racing by and you will know just why
Although I really had to leave and failed to say goodbye
There was no need, I am still close, I really did not die

*Terence Richardson, Denton*

Born in Brighton **Terence Richardson** began writing poetry in 1994 when he returned to education. "My work is influenced by the way I feel and I would describe my style as serious," he said. "I would like to be remembered as a caring man." Aged 51, he is a mature student with an ambition to settle in Ireland, write poetry and be happy. He has two grown up children and his hobbies include reading and creative writing. He has written many poems but this is the first one he has had published. "I have also written many essays," he added.

## SUTTON'S UNEXPLODED BUCKET

An unexploded bomb?
In Sutton, what a shock
I had to tell my mum
As she lives just round the block

They all got a tin hat
And the kids a day off school
I also liked the fact
There was free tea and coffee for all

The army dug a hole
But only found a rusty bucket
One soldier said, "oh blow"
But another said, "oh fur goodness sake"

So all a waste of time then
And everyone went home
Still, in the hole they could put a garden
With flowers and a gnome

*C Mappley, Carshalton*

## MAIN STATION MAELSTROM

Outward pours the throng from train
Into Suttons streets again
Milling, motivated swarm
Hurly-burly, haste the norm
Drawn by one magnetic pull
They see borough blossoms full
Of culture, commerce, the lot
Just like bees round honey pot
The mass materialises
Eagerness emphasises
Findings of the connoisseur
Sleepy malingerers stir
Wafted wisely throwley way
Others kind of homage pay
Spirits lifted by the maze
(How many more shopping days?)
Sutton sucks them in alright

Flames of fortune, fun ignite
Especially great elation
Pinpoints our railway station

*Ruth Daviat, Beddington*

## GOODBYE

There comes a time to say  goodbye
There comes a time to part
There will be no tears left to cry
All that will be left is a broken heart
But when all is over and done
And there's nothing left to give
There is no point in going on
And your own life you must start to live
It's best just to walk away
To try and forget the past
Pain is all you have if you stay
Because it's only memories that last

It's time to start afresh, head for pastures new
Just remember the one who wanted, it was you
If one day in the future you are all alone
Don't think about everything that's gone
It's no good looking back at what you had
When it's down to you that it all went bad
You had a life that was filled with love
But for you that wasn't good enough

*Debbie Gadd, Sutton*

## STILL - A RONDEAUX

I try to still my mind inside
It comes and goes, a beating tide
Sometimes so angry, spitting spray
A sea of troubled, heaving grey
My head's a storm, wind-blown, dark-eyed

If on a boat, salt in my hair
I could stand on the prow and dare
This wildness to wash over me?

I try to still

To jump is what my spirit craves
Surrender to those swaying waves
Singing their siren songs of shores
Which tell me through the mighty roars
Of soothing sands and sheltered caves
I try to...still

*Bewick Wilson, Essex*

## WELCOME

My train passed through Shalford this morning.
It slowed at the unmanned station
And I saw a new sign on the platform, "Welcome to Shalford".
Twenty years back there was always a welcome for us:
I would take the children to Shalford on the little train
And grandpa was waiting there, never late, always lovingly waiting
He bent to the children and swept them up with joy
Then he drove us home for a day in the country and woods
He showed them the toad in the cellar, the woodpeckers' nest and
the firewood
And read "The Just So Stories" or played with the bagatelle.

Not many trains stop at Shalford these days
And only a "Welcome", not welcome, remains for me there

*Elizabeth Woodhouse, Reigate*

## LICHENS

Little leafy living things
Abound on all our trees
On gates and posts and fences
Wherever air is free

Pollution kills these little plants
Which grace our house and ground
Their greys, their greens, their yellows
Then are never to be found

So guard your air and keep it clean
Protect these little plants

So future generations
Can take them to their hearts

*Rita Laundon, Morden*

## MALDON OF A THOUSAND YEARS AND MORE

Before there was an England here was Maeldune
From the easy rolling downs toward the bay
The carving of a wild blue estuary eastwards
The Blackwater, from the melt down and moraine
Parabolas of kelped green shallows, silent depths
On which the red sailed barges ply their salt
Whilst crests of natures own embroidery
Ride the waves with foaming truculence

The low shoreline with islets, jade sea grass
Grey shingle beach and pebble dappled reach
Barnacled remains of abandoned hulks like
Rotting carcasses of wilderbeEst
White flashing twitches signal sea birds, scavaging the
Shallows for a meal, their hungry cries pierce the ear

The golden morning sun thrusts her mottled sword
Towards the town, azure sky casts its dye into the sea
Patchwork fields, trees, lakes and fens, hythe quay
Parks and causeways come in view. Sails run aloft to
Catch the offshore breeze before the ebbing tide

Maldon of a thousand years, since Vikings came ashore

*Kevin Power, Maldon*

## THE DEATH OF EDGE

I awoke
And sensed immediately
That something was not right
It was the Death of Edge

Steely light shone through the streens
Cold moonbeams so cold and white

Although it was daylight
And I knew it was not right

A bird sang for it was paradise
And a plastic bag floated in a tree
And I knew it was not alright

For poor people mourned at
The Death of Edge
All night
And I knew it was not alright

*Frances Jessup, Haslemere*

## SECRETS AND INSIGHTS

Secrets and insights
Wisdom and love
All taken back by the hand from above
What was it for?
What does it mean?
Trees and grass wither, no longer green
The petals of a snowdrop, tender and new
Proud and hopeful, glistens with dew
Biting and snarling
Frost then doth claim
Winter creeps closer
And all is fair game
Life is lent to all
But we're the guests and not the host
Even springtime's lamb
Becomes the winters roast
Winter comes to all of us
Be it in season or in age
We're only tiny players on an
Ever changing stage

*A Cleary, Northolt*

## TANKA

The seabirds
Have returned at last
After all these months
Are they now
Hungrier for my eyes?

August
Sunlight
And the window of time

Grey poise
On a still white morning
One heron

*A A Marcoff, Epsom*

## DECISION TIME

See here that cracked roof tile
And from within, the angry sky
Dropping rain on my homely place,
Watch below all the while
The seeping damp no fire will dry
Enough to stop the rotting race

Such a small hole it is
Could be unnoticed for ever
But it's not insignificant
To the hostilities
Of the wild winds and wet weather.
Mans shelter seems impertinent.

Now is the time to act
To protect the house for a while
Safeguarding all those remaining.
A new tile is a fact.
The job will be done with a smile
And I'll start when it stops raining

*L Dale, Orpington*

A LONDON VISIT

I went to Covent Garden
Never been there before
It was so exciting - a new experience
Fresh, exuberant, an open door

No wonder the tourists flock there
So much for one to see
Markets, restaurants, pubs, quaint shops
Old buildings steeped in history

Young musicians playing music
A juggler tossing things in the air
An artist painting pictures
Happy faces everywhere

Thank you Covent Garden
For all you've given me
My heart is full of pride
For the feast my eyes did see

*Gladys C'Ailceta, Burgess Hill*

AVALON

There is a journey I must soon make
Following roads which only I may take
A time of searching, a spiritual quest
To look inside me, to find Lyonnesse
To see if I really do exist
To see what lies behind the veil of mist
To see where in the past I went wrong
To see the future, to find my Avalon
Somewhere amid the interminable void
Where infinity reaches farther and higher
Where everything is nothing, and all things are one
Brightly burns an unquenchable fire

*Dave Benham, Tadworth*

## FOOD FOR THE SOUL

The birds that sing from dawn 'till dusk
The genuine lore that comes after the lust
The startling stars that shine each night
Where there is darkness, soon will be light

A planted seed that grows each day
A gentle breeze, a tree to sway
A passing thought will always be there
A gift from above, for us all to share

Like the sea that continues to roll
These things have been given as food for the soul

*Marina O'Shea, Basildon*

## ENDURANCE

One can gain a stronger self from the pains and trials of life
Many miles we may travel from the cradle to the grave, while
The tested qualities of endurance can bring its owners honest
Rewards, to have hope that all pains and trials of this life, have
An end in sight, can bring relief to a sick and troubled mind
Hope can be based on the strong foundations of love, a hope for a
Better world to come, hope can believe all things, and hope itself
Will continue on
Amen

*Rowland Scannell, West Ewell*

## ODE TO DOVER CASTLE

High on the wonderful white cliffs of Dover
Stands a castle proud and bold
Through the centuries it has stood there
A magnificent sight to behold
Surrounded by trees of beautiful green
With blue skies overhead
It looks such a peaceful scene
But many a battle has been fought there
And shattered many a dream

People come from distant lands
Its history and glory to praise
God willing may it still be standing
Way out in the future distant days

*E Cornish, Dover*

## SMELL OF A MAN IN THE MORNING

Woke up to a September morning
The cold gap in my bed next to me
The pattern of the year returning
No first sound, no first cup of tea
No smell of a man in my bed
I look for crevasses to bury my head
But there's only space and pillow

Oh, but let go, let go
Of memories shaped by wanting
The truth is more of what I know
Mornings on eggshells, and shouting
Smells of vodka and fags
A huffy back turned to me
Is today when he'll pack his bags
Wondering when I'll be free

*Van Scharer, Sandwich*

## UPSTREAM

When eager youth was on my side
I was expansive wild and wide
In retrospect just a little - shallow

Years of experience I now keep
It makes me so profoundly deep
But unfortunately rather - narrow

*Richard Jones, Reigate*

## RESPECT YOUR PARENTS

Your parents have a job to do
When you're grown they want to be proud of you
They don't want to hang their heads in shame
Because you have disgraced their name

They would like to teach you love and respect
Not hooliganism and bullying
This couple whose love gave you birth
Won't want their good name sullying

Respect your parents, you know you should
It's much easier to be naughty than good
But it's so much better to keep your name clean
Then you'll be welcomed on every scene

Respect your parents, do what they say
No matter how much it offends
Then you'll grow up too. respected
Well loved by your family and friends

*Marjorie Wagg, Basildon*

## TIBBY

I am a cat named Tibby
My coat is black and white
When I stick my claws out
I give my mum a fright

I like to wash my coat
And make it gleam so bright
I also sharpen my claws
And get ready for the fight

I like to watch the water
Swirling in the sink
It gets me all excited
And then I stop to think

I like a game of ball
I kick it with my paws

When you go to grab it
I come out with my claws

I am such a happy cat
My people feed me fish
So when I have finished it
I like to clean my dish

*Linda Finch, Leigh-On-Sea*

LOVING LORD

You gave your son
The only one
Thy will be done
Oh, loving Lord

To forgive our sin
To heal the hurt within
To let our lives begin
Oh, loving Lord

You gave us your love
From heaven above
In the form of a dove
Oh, loving Lord

So, your name we will raise
With great songs of praise
For the rest of our days
Our loving Lord

*Tessa Bax, Ashford*

LONELINESS VERSUS HAPPINESS

Boxed in a shallow shell of image
Expectations round every corner
Substance lacking in my soul

On a self created odyssey
Without the tools of happiness
Tears form in a grown mans eye

To love someone is too easy
Happiness is created by a women
Loneliness is created by the quest

*N Kerry, Ashford*

FALLEN FLOWER

So young, she dropped and fell
And kissed the stony path
My golden daffodil of spring
O that I'd bound her stem
To stand erect
My lovely maiden flower
Now not to meet again
'Till next springs joyous hour

*Michael Rowson, Chichester*

EASTBOURNE EXPLAINED

The south of England is very sunny
But to buy things does cost lots of money

Eastbourne is a tourist town
With the sun trap of the south its crown

It's such a lovely place to stay
Whether permanently or just to play

Popular with the many old dears
As well as teenagers and their peers

For the kiddies there's so much to do
From Hampden Park to the local zoo

Fish and chips go down a treat
And ice-cream after is very neat

Grandma will love a game of bingo
If only she could learn the lingo
Maybe a tea dance would be better

Only if her arthritis will let her

There's a beautiful seafront and lots of shops
So much to do the fun never stops

And now you should be able to see
Why Eastbourne is the place to be

*Claire Shadwell, Eastbourne*

## APPROACHING ART

My finest words
But whisper
Of eternity

My clearest expression
Barely touch
The truth

And through rivers of ink
I must wade
In search of
Something
Approaching art

*Laurie Hilton-Ash, Brighton*

## PRAYER PLANT

Fragile, gentle plant
Pale green and tender
Each night you settle
Close your leaves in prayer
Do you, I wonder
Know to whom
It is that you render
Your silent homage?
The very word of life
Tells us that all creation
Waits for its redemption
So perhaps you know
In very truth

*K Bailes, Lewes*

## A LIFETIME FRIEND

A lifetime friend is very rare
But I have one who's more than fair
Many traumas we've been through
But lots of happy moments too

We call it an invisible bond
Of one another we are fond
No one can break this firm link
Too many years have passed we think

From schooldays to our golden years
From being young we're now old dears
For one another we are still there
Years have not changed the way we care

Come what may in days to come
We feel that we have really done
What many people would like to do
Be nice, sincere and above all true

*Sylvia Ash, Eastbourne*

## PROGRESS

Millions of pixels striving for graphical perfection
Everyday shape hiding your technological brilliance
Systematic approach, no madness to your method

Superior worker you're the cause of the shorter week
The ultimate employee, no scruples, opinions or complaints
Ruler of the universe, business markets are nothing minus your help
But you are a slave to electricity
A social addict to power
You are nothing at the pull of a plug
Who says computers are getting out of control?

*Suzanne Mudd, Grays*

# DIFFERENT QUALITIES, DIFFERENT TIMES

Different qualities, different times
Pressure points along these lines
And memories fade and rise sometimes
With different qualities at different times

An impression left for another day
Of what past history had to say
It could all pop up another way
When left to do as it may

Violet the gardener saw herself grow
She rested, fed, gave such a show
What do the other gardeners know
Of where they are about to go?

Autumnal cycle wearing thin
Laughing hyacinths now begin
Market gardeners begin to sing
Another petal falls in the bin

Different qualities, different times
Pressure points along these lines
And memories, reflections, dreams come true
A winter cycle points to you

*Clive Marks, Orpington*

# CHANGING MOODS

Just now I'm in a tranquil mood
Creeping up the beach in gentle ripples
Waves fringed like scalloped lace
Yachtsmen are frustrated and becalmed
Sunlight reflects as sparkling sapphires
Playfully dancing over me

Suddenly, dark clouds scud across the sky
Seagulls cry, ride my choppy waves
I dash huge waves upon the rocks
Toss pebbles up like shuttlecocks

The unwary I drench with spray
Laughter echoes along the bay

Sometimes I hear the lifeboats claxon sound
Maybe I've caused a ship to go aground
Sandcastles have all been washed away
Spotless sand awaits another day
I'd like to be gentle, not heave and roll
But my changing moods are not in my control

*Iris Owen, Eastbourne*

ASHFORD

London: Ashford: Paris
Wester Ross and Harris.
The Euro and Diana's death.
The Railway Works' last dying breath.

*Alan Lavender, Ashford*

MY POEM

Bewitched by life
Like tempestuous sea
Every day plays havoc with me
Bitter winds of change
Bewilder, but amaze
Steely moon, hits sun rays

And even as life
Sucks all energy
It pulls on heart strings
Some ray of hope
In the big scope of things
Suddenly hits hard
Between the real and soft dreams
Stars shake their glitter
As foxes root through night litter

Confessions will dart, many and few
All the old was once new

Wishes ah, wishes, wishes, wishes
I'm told come true

*Julie Sexton, Haslemere*

## A FISHY WISH

If I was granted just one wish
I would find a bank and fish and fish
And if I did not get a bite
I would sit around for day and night
My hobby brings me perfect peace
Except for quacks from ducks and geese
Wordly cares would be put aside
My aches and pains I'm sure would hide
When I'm sitting alongside a stream
Tranquil pictures fill my dream
At times I have a lucky strike
I'd think I caught a ten-stone pike
Awake.....I've hooked a tiny newt
And he's inside a worn-out boot
Today I'm glum and catching nowt
The river's dry......a bloody drought

*Tom Chilton, Hove*

## SAY CHEESE

He did not stay to develop the future
He was out of the picture
Gone in a flash
My red eyes - witness - of unguarded shock
My mouth a perfect aperture of surprise
And with the force of his departure
All sense of focus was so shaken
Hopes blurred and
Memories superimposed
In impossible configurations
Not only had he torn the final pages from our album
But - in moving on
The negatives of our past
Were left - to me

*J A Karpinska, Hove*

MOTHER, MY INSPIRATION

You are my desire to live
You fill me with pride
I love you dear mother, yes I do

We have had our differences
We have spoken foolish words
But our love is so strong we will not
Break apart
I feed on that security and
Supported by the love
Take away my mother, I am helpless
She is my hope

No words can ever draw a picture image of
What I feel
It is said, actions speak louder than words
And in this case I think it is true

What ever you feel or think mother
I need you and always will
Please know that
You are the inspiration of my life

*Ms Kerry, London*

ANCIENT SEA ROVERS

From the northlands came the Vikings
Came the warriors seeking land
In there long boats mighty menfolk
Drawn from every creek and strand

They were men who knew the cruel seas
Though their boats were many manned
Braved all rigours sent to harm them
Leapt and cheered on all new sand

How they wandered, pillaged, plundered
Nothing safe from clutching hand
Till our king the mighty Alfred

Pushed them north the way he'd planned

Still they spread as time permitted
Though their way was often banned
Some they settled north in Scotland
Others Greenland and Iceland

New worlds opened up before them
As each leader raised his hand
Common sense though harsh provided
Fortitude at every  stand

J Fermor, Peacehaven

## THOUGHTS OF A LOVELY JUNE

Where summer fades and autumn falls
And winter calls to soon
Dreams linger in the morning mist
Thoughts of a lovely June

A whisper on the wings of love
Whose heart will search for thee
A gentle kiss, a sweet caress
A precious memory

A fleeting touch, a moment past
A place, a friendly room
In quiet repose a transient bloom
Thoughts of a lovely June

June Pledger, Grays

## MY JOURNEY OF ENLIGHTENMENT

I'm on a journey to a better place
Where my problems and anxieties I must face
A journey that is hard and long
I cannot falter, I must be strong
A lot of things will have to change
My whole life I'll have to rearrange
Turn negative to positive, wrong to right

Bad to good and dark to light
I cannot sit back and procrastinate
And leave it all till it's too late
I must see it through to the bitter end
And then my life I can start to mend

*Vanessa Galloway, Surrey*